Love

Remember how powerful a photograph can be.

More powerful than any bombs.

As powerful as love.

[KIM PHUC]

M·I·L·K™

MOMENTS INTIMACY LAUGHTER KINSHIP

This edition published in 2004 by WPL, The Perfume Factory,
140 Wales Farm Road, London W3 6UG.
www.wpl.eu.com

Edited and designed by WPL
Printed in China

ISBN 1-904264-35-2

Inspired by the 1950s landmark photographic exhibition, "The Family of Man", M.I.L.K. began as an epic global search to develop a collection of extraordinary and geographically diverse images portraying humanity's Moments of Intimacy, Laughter and Kinship (M.I.L.K.). This search took the form of a photographic competition – probably the biggest and almost certainly the most ambitious of its kind ever to be conducted. Chosen from 40,000 entries worldwide, the 300 winning images cut across race and nationality and celebrate what it is to be part of a family, to share the gift of friendship and more than anything else, to be loved.

These photographs were first published as three books entitled "Family", "Friendship" and "Love" in early 2001 and are now featured in a range of products worldwide, in nine different languages in more than 20 countries. M.I.L.K. is also a travelling exhibition.

There is only one happiness in life,
to *love* and be loved.

[GEORGE SAND]

Love does not consist in gazing at each other

but in looking outward together

in the same direction.

[ANTOINE SAINT-EXUPERY]

Love is just a word until someone you meet

gives it a proper meaning.

It is hard to pinpoint

the exact moment love begins

but it is easier to recognise that it has begun.

'Tis one thing to be tempted,

another thing to fall.

[SHAKESPEARE]

One man all by himself is nothing.

Two people who belong together
make a world.

[HANS MARGOLIUS]

Love is composed of a single soul

inhabiting two bodies.

[ARISTOTLE]

When you're in love
you smile on the inside and out.

To the world you may be just one person

but to one person you may be the world.

Love is a sharing of pleasures
and a merging of souls.

Grow old along with me,
the best is yet to be.

Love sees not with the eyes

but with the mind.

Falling in love is easy

but **staying** in love

is something very special.

Do you love me because I am beautiful

or am I beautiful because you love me ?

We can do no great things –

only small things with great love.

[MOTHER TERESA]

True love produces a perfect match.

Love is when you're still *dancing*
long after the music has stopped.

You will find as you look back upon your life

that the moments when you have truly lived

are the moments when you have done things

.in the spirit of love.

[HENRY DRUMMOND]

A heart that truly loves is forever young.

In the mathematics of love,

you minus me = nothing

but you plus me = everything.

Love is more than the entanglement of two hearts, it is the entwining of two lives, forever.

It takes a minute to have a crush on someone,

an hour to like someone

and a day to love someone...

but it takes a lifetime to forget someone.

Love at first sight is easy to understand.

It's when two people have been

looking at each other for years

that it becomes a miracle.

[SAM LEVENSON]

Love makes the world go round.

M.I.L.K. IMAGES

A boy places a protective arm around his young companion during a walk in the park in London, England – 1937.
© Walter Bellamy / Getty images

Holding hands in the surf – an elderly couple get away from it all on Sandy Hook beach in New Jersey, USA.
© Y Nagasaki

A cheeky young couple distracts Alfonso from his newspaper as he waits for his bus in Barcelona, Spain.
© David Sanchez Gimenez

Joe's special relationship with his wife is obvious to visitors to his shoe repair shop in Covina, California, USA.
© J D Nielsen

Putting your feet up takes on a new meaning in Indiana, USA.
© Richard Frank

Waiting patiently – in a remote fishing village in Southern Chile, bar owners Mr and Mrs Andrade ponder when their next customer will arrive.
© Paz Errázuriz

A peaceful moment at the Zen Mountain Monastery on Mount Tremper, in the state of New York, USA.
© Karen Maini

Boy meets girl – in the small village of Kižinga in Southern Siberia, Russia.
© Jindřich Štreit

Rain delays the beginning of carnival in Barahona, Dominican Republic. A young couple exchange a flirtatious glance as they wait for the festivities to begin.
© Tino Soriano

On a journey through the steppes of Inner Mongolia in China, new friends pause to feed their horses and to share a moment of quiet affection.
© Everett Kennedy Brown

The spirit of the old Latin American phrase "tienes luz en la pupila" – "you have light in your eyes" – is captured in this photograph of Putulungo and Alma, taken in Portobelo, Panama.
© Sandra Eleta

On the streets of Santiago de Cuba, Cuba – a couple's uninhibited display of affection raises a spontaneous smile from their young audience.
© Mikhail Evstafiev

As the parade passes by in the Rio de Janeiro carnival, Brazil, a young couple share an affectionate kiss amid the crowd.
© Marcio RM

Young lovers clasp each other tight as they dance to the rhythms of Havana, Cuba.
© Vincent Delbrouck

Newly wedded bliss on Long Island, New York, USA – Travis catches Camille's wedding veil when it blows off in the wind, but he can't resist trying it on before returning it to his new wife.
© Renate Pfleiderer

In their own world – on a crowded subway train in New York, USA, a young couple only have eyes for each other.
© Christophe Agou

The 60th wedding anniversary - love, respect and six decades of marriage bind husband and wife Henri and Violet Mayoux. They exchange a humorous look as they prepare to cut their anniversary cake in Ontario, Canada.
© Ricardo Ordóñez

On a pedestal – a farmer looks up to his wife in the rural village of Ruseni, Romania.
© Robert Lifson

Bob drives his wife, Peggy, home to Houston, Texas, USA. The couple have been married for 54 years.
© Todd Davis

Two kilted friends stand out from the crowd at the Gay Pride Festival in London, England.
© Davy Jones

After a swim in the chilly waters of a Moscow river, a Russian couple steal the show with a display of affection.
© Vladimir Kryukov

Arm in arm - sharing sunshine and shopping on a day trip to Manly, a seaside suburb of Sydney, Australia.
© David Hancock

A train station in Tallinn, Estonia, is the setting for tearful farewells as sailors from the Russian fleet say goodbye to their Estonian girlfriends.
© Piotr Malecki

Outdoor pursuit – a park bench makes a change from the sofa for an elderly couple winding a ball of wool in Prague, Czech Republic.
© Josef Sekal

A young girl gazes with interest at an attractive young man on a sunlit street in Apithia, Greece.
© Tommy Agriodimas

The photographer captured this affectionate image of his grandfather Max, 86, and grandmother Ann, 80, in New Port Richie, Florida, USA.
© Sam Devine Tischler

The usual routine – side by side, an elderly couple patiently wait for their washing to dry. They are residents of Sun City Arizona, a retirement community in the USA.
© Al Lieberman